D0862730

JUMBO JACK'S COOKBOOKS
AUDUBON MEDIA CORPORATION
301 BROADWAY • AUDUBON IA 50025
1-800-798-2635

LOST AND BURIED
TREASURE
OF
THE MISSISSIPPI RIVER

by
Netha Bell
and Gary Scholl

Quixote Press
31798 K18S
Sioux City, Iowa
51109

i

* * * * * * * * * *

QUIXOTE
PRESS

Bruce Carlson
31798 K18S
Sioux City, IA
51109

Printed
in
the
U.S.A.

iii

DEDICATIONS

Dedicated to the memory of my father, Oliver William Scholl, who in his own way was a treasure seeker, making his fortune by hard work and true and honest living. He found his gold mine in his family and the people who loved him.

Gary Scholl

I would like to dedicate my part of the book to my husband, Lowell Bell, and my son, Jim Albert, who have been so patient with me during my research.

Netha Bell

TABLE OF CONTENTS

PREFACE 11

CHAPTERS

The reader must appreciate the fact that none of these stories have ever been published before. Some of them could cause embarrassment to living people today. Because of that, some of the stories use fictitious names. In those cases, it should be understood that any similarity between those names and actual people, living or dead, is purely coincidental.

ACKNOWLEDGEMENTS

I want to acknowledge my wife, Sandy's, help in retyping my manuscript and organizing the illustrations into book form.

I also want to acknowledge our dear friend and co-author, Netha Bell's contribution for the original illustrations and the hours of work involved in compiling all the data for the book.

Gary Scholl

I would like to thank all of the ladies at both the Cattermole and Idol Rashid Libraries, and in particular, Rose Reynolds, Ethel Richman and Chris Cowles, for all their help.

Netha Bell

PREFACE

Truth or legend? Fact or fiction? You be the judge. Go with us to the days of prospectors, outlaws, renegade Indians and river pirates. Follow age-old treasure maps in search of gold and other treasures left behind by those people.

Stare into the eyes of a shady-looking riverboat gambler aboard a majestic paddle wheeler as you lay your hand of aces and eights on the table.

Explore the dark, cold depth of old caves and mines in search of hidden fortunes.

Live with the people of the times, and go with them on their quests for fame and fortune.

For these are the lost and perhaps still-buried treasures of the Mississippi River.

CHAPTER I

THE EDDYVILLE TREASURE

The settlement of Eddyville, Iowa, is the site of an old Indian village and trading post.

In 1903, W.W. DeLong, then postmaster of Eddyville, received a letter postmarked, Pittsburgh, Pennsylvania. The letter was addressed simply: Postmaster, Eddyville, Iowa, and signed, Le Barge.

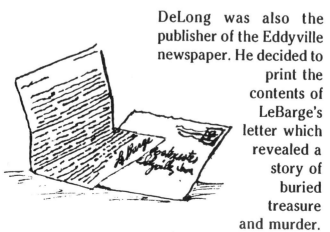

DeLong was also the publisher of the Eddyville newspaper. He decided to print the contents of LeBarge's letter which revealed a story of buried treasure and murder.

LeBarge and two others had struck it rich while prospecting for gold in the Black Hills. In the summer of 1878, they were passing through the Eddyville area on their way to Illinois, where they lived. Each of the men carried a gallon jug, full of gold dust and nuggets. The value of the gold at the time was estimated at some twenty-five thousand dollars.

One night, a camp site was chosen at a bend in the trail about a mile north of Eddyville. After finishing their evening meal, they settled down to a game of poker. One of the men known as William Gunton came out a

heavy winner. Not taking his losses lightly, LeBarge accused him of cheating and a fight broke out. During the confrontation, Gunton was stabbed and killed.

The victim's head was cut off and thrown into the campfire, while the headless body was dragged some distance away and buried.

(14)

The remaining two men knew that if they were ever caught with all the gold in their possession they would certainly be accused of killing Gunton for his share of the gold. The two men then decided to bury the jugs of gold in three different locations, using the grave as marker.

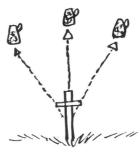

They then continued their journey, planning to return at some later date to reclaim the gold. By that time there would be little, if any, evidence to connect them with the crime.

Saying in his letter that he was about to die, LeBarge asked the postmaster to recover Gunton's body and give it a decent burial. He also asked that the gold be given to the men taking care of the services.

Three men, DeLong, Sid Crosson and Arthur Beamer, set out in search of the gold.

Although the letter gave a detailed description of the place where the gold was supposed to be, nothing was ever found and a few days later the search was called off.

The story of the buried treasure was all but forgotten until 1920, when a road crew grading the old wagon trial north of Eddyville uncovered a human skull that showed evidence of having been burned.

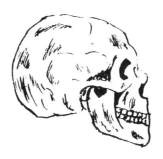

DeLong insisted that the skull had been found in almost the exact location described in LeBarge's letter. The news of the discovery drew hundreds of treasure hunters to the area just north of the Eddyville Cemetery.

To this day, no traces of the gold has ever been found. Perhaps the ghost of Gunton still guards the secret to its whereabouts.

CHAPTER II

THE HAUNTED HEARTHSTONE

ear the now abandonded town of Hauntstown, Illinois, comes the tale of the hanuted hearthstone.

Rumor has it that Jessie Barnes had made a quite sizable fortune in the lumber business. Most people in the early 1900's didn't trust banks or bankers, and they kept their money and other valuables at home and hidden.

Barnes was not a very neighborly individual and very seldom let anyone, other than trusted friends, any further than the front door of his cabin.

Many years before he moved to Hauntstown, his wife had passed away during childbirth, and he had never remarried. As far anyone knew, old Jessie had no living relatives. When Jessie Barnes died, the tales of a fortune either hidden in the cabin or buried somewhere nearby brought many people to the area in search of Jessie's cache, but they never found it.

One night several years later the old cabin mysteriously burned to the ground before anyone could reach it in time to put the fire out.

This, however, did not deter four people from nearby Hardin from continuing the search for the fortune. One of them, Elizabeth Petrie, had been to a fortune teller. During the session, the fortune teller told Elizabeth that she was destined to come into a large sum of money.

She was also told that this money could be found buried beneath a hearthstone. By the dark of night, Elizabeth and three male companions, took off for Jessie's cabin even though it looked like it might rain. The cabin was located on an old dirt road a considerable distance from the main road and the

four went bouncing along in the old Model A Touring Car.

Armed with two shovels and a corn planter stake, they got right to work. By using the corn planter stake as a lever they were finally able to begin moving the hearthstone. It took several hours to get the heavy stone moved only a few inches. They still hadn't moved it enough to do any digging before they abandonded the project for fear that the coming rain would leave them stranded back

there in the woods. Thunder rolled and the lightning flashed as they left as fast as they could.

The next day a neighbor of Jessie's, J.D. Houston, went to see where the lightning had hit. When he got to the remains of Jessie's cabin, he found things just as they had always been. Unbeknownst to him the lightning had moved the hearthstone back to its original position.

Could Mother Nature be trying to keep this treasure hidden?

As far as anyone knows, Elizabeth and her friends never returned to the cabin to continue their search and it is believed that nobody else has ever recovered Jessie's fortune.

If, however, the fortune teller was right about the location of the money, it is still there, under the haunted hearthstone.

CHAPTER III

BRACKEN'S CACHE

 uring the early days of the Civil War, around 1862, a treasure of considerable value, and believed to be mostly in gold, was buried by a Minnesota settler, John Bracken. It is said to be buried either on or near the grounds of the present Minnesota Old Soldiers' Home.

Because of the war and the wide widespread uncertainty of the economy at the time, Bracken no doubt considered it to be the safest way to hang onto his fortune.

Legend has it that the burial spot was on the west bank of the Mississippi River, near what is now the southern city limits of Minneapolis.

According to several stories, it is said that Bracken just seemed to have forgotten about the buried gold for many years.

Bracken's health began to fail in his early 80's, and he knew he was about to die. In a deathbed statement to a close friend named Paul Johnson, Bracken finally revealed the story of his buried treasure. Apparently, however, he was not too sure of the exact location. Following Bracken's Death, Johnson made several unsuccessful attempts to locate the gold. Knowing that he may not ever find the gold alone, Johnson confided in another friend, Bill Parker, and told him the whole story.

Absolutely certain that he knew where the gold was, Parker asked for permission to dig at the spot where he believed the treasure to be located. By this time, though, the property had come into the hands of the state, and permission was denied.

Permission to do much of anything on state-owned land, especially treasure hunting, is still required from the top brass, and perhaps someday, Bracken's cache will be found.

CHAPTER IV

WEST OF SINGLETON'S BARN

uring the Sioux Indian uprising, from 1862 to 1864 in Minnesota, many families of white settlers were completely wiped out. The Indians often burned every home, outbuilding, and stand of trees and timber that had anything at all to do with a white man.

In most cases, there was not time for the people  to bury or hide their valuables, which were carried off by the Indians. It is known, however, that several families, having been warned ahead of time that the Indians were on a rampage were able to hide sums of money, jewelry, and other valuables before fleeing the troubled area.

There are several recorded cases of two or three family members returning to their once-happy homes, to find the charred ruins of their farms.  Everything they had remembered to use as a landmark was destroyed, giving them little, if any, clues to the whereabouts of the things they had left behind.

One such family was that of John Singleton, who had lived in Wabasha County.

Singleton and his family had moved from Kentucky to settle in Minnesota. Through hard work and shrewd trading, he made a sizable fortune for the times, which he kept at his home. The story goes, that at the first news of the Indian uprising, Singleton, fearing that the family would be caught and the money taken from them, took a shovel and all his valuables and set out to find a safe place to bury them. It is said that he went straight west of his barn forty yards to a stand of small trees and buried his cache.

He later said that if he had to be gone awhile, that the trees would still be there as a marker.

All but three of the family members were killed before they could reach safety. A few months after the Indian trouble was at least partly settled, John Singleton and his two sons returned to the farm site. Imagine their surprise to find that everything had changed! All the buildings and surrounding timber had been badly burned or totally destroyed.

This combined with the loss of his family nearly destroyed Singleton's mind. He was unable to locate the money and other valuables that  would have enabled him to re-establish the farm.

All he could ever tell his sons was that he had gone west of the barn to a grove of trees and buried the strong box. Since the trees had been burned so badly, the markers he had used were destroyed and the cache was never found.

CHAPTER V

FLOOD LEVELS GHOST TOWN

he Great Flood of 1851 left in its path a lot of death and destruction over the entire Mississippi Valley.

The booming riverport town of Burris City was virtually wiped clean of any human life, and the seventy or so empty buildings of the once-flourishing city now reflect only memories of the past.

The now empty town soon became a haven for outlaws and river pirates. It is believed that, perhaps, Jesse James and his gang once spent some time there while on a train-

robbing spree in the area. They are suspected of at least once robbing the CB & Q (Chicago, Burlington and Quincy) railroad and stashing the loot in a cave somewhere along the river.

Burris City is located on the north side of the Iowa River at its junction with the Mississippi, in Louisa County, Iowa.

The river pirates of the day were said to have buried a lot of gold, silver, and other valuables throughout the town and surrounding area.

As late as 1960, a treasure hunter combing the town in search of something valuable, struck it rich when he uncovered a fortune in gold buried under a big oak tree on a back street in the city.

The gold coins that were in the exceptional find were from a California mint which made them even more valuable.

CHAPTER VI

McGREGOR'S GOLD

ust before dark one chilly fall evening in 1843, a federal pay master and two guards stopped for the night at an inn in northeast Iowa. The paymaster was a tall, lanky man around fifty years old. He was heavily armed, and with good reason. Each of his saddle-bags contained two canvas bags marked U.S. Government. These four bags are said to have

contained sixty-three thousand dollars in gold coins. This money was the back pay for the soldiers stationed at several wilderness forts on the western prairies.

As the men finished their supper, the paymaster suddenly jumped to his feet, clutched his chest and cried out, "I . . . I think I'm gonna die, . . . I'm gonna die."

He grabbed the money bags from beside his chair and threw them over his shoulder. Doubled over and coughing, he ordered the two guards not to follow him and disappeared into the night. It is said that only ten minutes had passed before he returned. He appeared in the doorway and collapsed on the floor . . . dead.

The gold was gone.

Fortune hunters have been searching for the gold for about a century and a half, but none of it has been recovered.

Some residents of the area are amused by the constant attempts by fortune hunters to find the treasure, but most of the folks around McGregor are convinced that the story is true.

The actual happenings at the inn came from the innkeeper, but they never told why the man had died. It seemed to be common knowledge that the paymaster had always felt that the two guards with him were not to be trusted. Some say that they poisoned his supper, but others say that the man had a heart condition and that the day's ride, combined with the heavy supper, brought on a fatal heart attack.

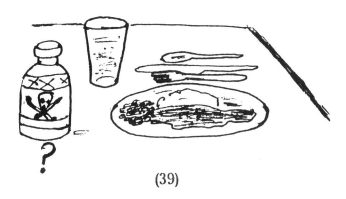

Old yarn spinners still claim that the paymaster was gone only ten minutes and that his guards stayed behind while he hid the gold. Whatever happened to the two guards after that night is unknown. It is believed that they split up and went their separate ways without ever finding the gold.

Had the dying messenger been away from the inn more than ten minutes, the story would certainly be less appealing. But, within a five-minute walk in any direction from the original site of the inn, there was only one logical hiding place. This was a large cave, now located on a farm, owned at that time by an ancestor of the present owners, and it is a few miles west of McGregor, Iowa.

In 1843, this was a large cave, but erosion has filled it in so that today all that one can see is a shoveled-scarred sink hole where the cave used to be, with a gaping hole in the bottom.

The hole itself appears bottomless; and since no one has been in that sink hole for over seventy years, it is not known just how deep it really is. The large and small holes left all around the cave area are reminders of the untold hours spent digging in search of the treasure.

When William Meyer first bought the farm with the legend about the gold in 1887, his own curiosity prompted him to check the story against federal documents. Official government records did reveal that a payroll had, indeed, been lost on what is now the Meyer property. The record further stated that the loss was in the amount of sixty-three thousand dollars, with no record of it ever being recovered.

Assuming that the money had already been found, Meyer set about making a living as a farmer with hard work and long hours.

Although his five sons were never encouraged to look for the lost treasure, boys will be boys, and they and several other young neighbors undertook the task of descending into the depths of the cave.

After lowering themselves on ropes to a depth of some sixty feet, they found what they were sure was the floor of the hole that was only about a hundred feet in length, going absolutely nowhere. They found nothing else but total darkness and a damp, musty odor.

The legend of the lost gold has received considerable attention in recent years. One of the most persistent of these fortune hunters was a farmer and spiritualist, who came to the area about every six months throughout a ten-year period. This rare individual spent the first part of each visit in the old timers' section of a nearby cemetery. Hunched on a tombstone, he said that he was able to communicate with the dead.

He hoped that those who were alive in 1843 would know where the gold was hidden. After falling into a deep trance for an hour or so, he would race to the site of the old mine and dig feverishly as long as his strength would permit.

Old age finally caught up with him and stopped

his sporadic digging, but he never lost faith in his ability to communicate with the dead.

Many others have looked for the treasure. Their searching began shortly after the gold was lost and continues every year.

Another story growing out of the original legend claims that some years ago a team of government searchers came to the area armed with a special gold-locating machine.

They tried their machine about two miles from the cave, and the pointer led them to the exact spot where so many others had hunted for the gold. Like the others, they dug energetically through tree roots, rocks and deposits of sandstone. Their luck was better than average. It is said that they found a battered old gold watch. After finding the watch, they abandoned their search.

Most of those familiar with the tales of buried gold in Iowa are content to make their living in more conventional ways, but it may be that the appeal of gold to the Iowans of a century ago may still linger in some of the treasure seekers of today.

CHAPTER VII

RIVER CITY MADE FAMOUS

he city of Hannibal, on the Mississippi River in northeast Missouri, was made famous by the very distinguished novelist, Mark Twain. Many well-known landmarks in the Hannibal area are described in detail in his writings. The famous books, HUCKLEBERRY FINN and TOM SAWYER, are legendary, to say the least.

Mark Twain had a deep fascination for the great Mississippi and at one point in his  life acquired a pilot's license and navigated a steamboat up and down the river.

Hannibal and the surrounding river bluffs of the Mississippi are famous for other things as well.

There are a couple of well-known caves through out the area, but the two best known are Mark Twain and McDowell's Cave.

Legend has it that there is a ton of gold bars buried somewhere in the hills between Mark Twain Cave and the river. The gold is believed to have been salvaged from a river wreck during the Civil War and hidden by the men of the salvage crew.

It is also said that there is a large amount of gold hidden in or buried somewhere near McDowell's Cave.

Legend also states that during the Black Hawk

Wars, the famous Indian chief had stolen thousands of dollars worth of gold and silver and hid the loot in a cave in the river bluffs near Hannibal.

Finding such a treasure may be as simple as casting a watchful eye on the river bluffs as you cruise up and down the Great Mississippi.

CHAPTER VIII

THE GREAT RACE

nder a clear night sky in May, 1837, THE BEN SHARROD, on her weekly trip up river, overtook THE PRAIRIE just a few miles south of St. Louis. Not wanting to be passed, THE PRAIRIE stoked her boilers to the limit and the race to the next dock was on.

Feeding her fires with fast, hot-burning pitchwood and resin, THE SHARROD slowly crept ahead. The race had lasted nearly five miles before the intense heat from the boilers of THE SHARROD set fire to sixty cords of wood stacked alongside them.

As the pilot steered for the shore, several explosions from barrels of brandy, whiskey and gun powder threw two hundred passengers and crew into the river.

Now, with the wheel jammed and the pressure valves closed, the twin boilers erupted in a final massive explosion, tearing the remainder of the boat in half and sending her to the bottom of the Mighty Mississippi.

When THE COLUMBUS came along, over half of THE SHARROD'S people had already been killed by the blasts or drowned. The crew from The Columbus took aboard the survivors they could find in the dark water.

Since they had only the moon and torches for light, it is believed that some survived the blasts but drowned because they couldn't be seen.

One survivor was rescued by the steamer, STATESMAN, after floating some fifteen miles down the river. He told an incredible story of losing the entire assets of a Louisiana bank that had been entrusted to him for opening an out-of-state bank in Minnesota.

THE SHARROD went down with two strong boxes containing one hundred thousand dollars in gold.

Several efforts during the next two years to find

the wreckage of THE SHARROD and the hundred thousand dollars proved fruitless. The Mississippi mud still holds the secret of the final resting place of all that gold.

CHAPTER IX

PHONY MONEY

ear the mouth of the Wisconsin River where it empties into the Mississippi, between the towns of Gotham and Port Andrews, is a bluff that for years has been known as Bogus Bluff. In the 1800's at the bottom of this bluff was a cave, its entrance covered by thick underbrush and trees.

Everyone called it Counterfeiters' Cave.

Though the opening to the cave was small, a tunnel led back into the rock several feet, then opened up into a large cavern. It is said that the cavern was big enough that a grown man, without fear of hitting his head, could stand upright in it.

The bluff and cave got their names back in the late 1800's when a band of counterfeiters, led by a man named Ellis, was operating in the area. They used the cave as their base of operation where, by lantern light, they made the counterfeit money, mostly coins. They would exchange the counterfeit money for the real thing, then return to the cave where they would hide the real money. It is not known just how long this counterfeiting ring operated before they were caught in a town of Boscobel. The counterfeiters were sent to jail, thus putting an end to their operation. In the cave there may still be money laying around. If there is, whether it's the real thing or counterfeit is not known. Whatever it is, it could still be of value to collectors and historians.

Also about this time, a boat going to Fort Winnebago was robbed by a gang of outlaws. On board the boat at the time was not only the payroll for the soldiers but also a large amount of gold. The outlaws

made it as far as the bluff before they decided to hide their ill-gotten gains so they could travel more easily and make their escape.

It is believed that the gang was caught before they had a chance to return and recover their fortune.

To this day, Bogus Bluff and Counterfeiter's Cave hold not one but perhaps two treasures.

CHAPTER X

BLACK HAWK

n the pages of our history books, we find detailed accounts of minor clashes, major battles, and all-out war between the Indians and the white men.

Courageous men and women who believed in the westward movement, and the expansion of the country, died at the hands of great war chiefs of the Indian nations. But those early men of the plains also died in a hopeless effort to keep the white man from taking the land. A prime example would be what happened on the Little Big Horn River in Montana. There was a bitterly fought battle between  General Custer with the 7th Cavalry and Chief Crazy Horse and men from the entire Sioux Nation.

The Mississippi Valley also had its own great war chief. Chief Black Hawk, chief of the Sac tribe, led most of the fighting in the southeastern Iowa area of the river.

In 1813, Black Hawk and his warriors laid seige to the fort of Fort Madison. The soldiers and few civilians ran for their lives for fear of being captured or killed and left the fort in the hands of Black Hawk. The Indians looted the place taking with them most anything of value, especially the white man's gold.

One account states that Black Hawk buried some fifty thousand dollars in gold coins somewhere in the hills near what is now the town of Denmark, west of highway X-32 in Lee County.

Another account says that about this same time,

Black Hawk and several of his braves buried a large amount of gold on the north side of the Des Moines River in the northwestern corner of Davis County. The site of one large cache is believed to be in Section 2, Township 70, Range 12, of Davis County.

To this day, there is no positive proof that any of this gold has ever been recovered.

As absolute proof that people change with the times, historians tell us that Chief Black Hawk was the guest of honor at the Fourth of July celebration at Fort Madison in 1838. The speech he gave proved to be his farewell address, as he died in October that same year.

Black Hawk's original burial site was in the Iowaville cemetery just west of Selma, Iowa, on highway 16 in Davis County.

CHAPTER XI

A TEARFUL FAREWELL

 aul Goodwin had worked in his father's store almost as long as he could remember. He started on the ground floor sweeping and stocking the lower shelves with the small items he could handle and worked his way up waiting on customers, stocking the upper shelves and even ordering items to replace the ones they had sold.

Within a year after Paul and Virginia married, his father, Harry, started talking about opening another store up north.

Up north could refer to almost anyplace since they lived in St. Louis, Missouri.

On Paul and Virginia's fifth wedding anniversary, Harry decided that it was time for the move and finally put a name to the place up north, La Crosse, Wisconsin. He wanted Paul and Virginia to take their two children and move to La Crosse so Paul could run the store; after all, Paul had been running the store almost by himself for the past year.

After much talking, not only between Harry and Paul, but also between Paul and Virginia, Paul decided to take his father up on his offer. Plans were set in motion.

By the end of winter, all the plans were finalized. All they needed to wait for was the opening of the river to boat traffic so they could get their belongings to La Crosse.

Late in May of 1857, everything was ready. One-way tickets had been bought on THE ADAMS. All their household goods were packed as well as the inventory that Paul planned to take with him to open the store. Harry had decided it would take less time to get the store going if Paul took half of the stock from the store in St. Louis, and he would replace it. Harry also gave Paul a deer-hide bag containing thousands of dollars in gold coins.

June 1, 1857, was the day for tearful goodbyes as Paul, Virginia and their two children waited on the dock until the very last minute before boarding THE ADAMS. Harry and his wife, Sarah, along with Virginia's parents, William and Mary Stewart, were there to see them off. You know how it is when folks leave home; everyone hugs everyone, all the women cry and the children look as if they aren't really sure just what's going on. It's even worse if it's an only child who is leaving and it's the first time he has been away from home for any length of time. For some reason, it almost seems even harder if it's a daughter that's leaving.

Finally the time had come. The four Goodwins walked up the gangplank, found a place by the rail-

ing and waited. Before long, the boat started moving. Everyone waved, the women put hankies to their eyes, and the children clung to their mother's skirt.

The trip upriver was slow or maybe it just seemed slow since both children got sick.

Virginia had to spend most of her time in the cabin with the children, going up on deck only when Paul could stay with them, which was usually after they had been put to bed for the night. Then Virginia would stroll the decks for an hour or so or sit and talk with one of the other women on board.

After what seemed like years, they pulled into Oquawka, Illinois, for supplies and to pick up a few more passengers. This brought the total number of cabin passengers to fifteen.

While they were alongside the levee, Virginia decided to take the children ashore for a short walk, since they were feeling a bit better.

She thought maybe being on land would help.

The family boarded THE ADAMS not long before she blew her departing whistle. Her engines started and her paddles began to turn as she pulled away from the levee. No one will ever know exactly what happened next. All of a sudden, there was a big explosion in the boilers and parts of the boat blew in all directions.

It was reported that one part of the boat was sent flying toward town where it landed on the roof of a coffee house three blocks away. A piece of iron bar was sent hurling at such speed that it cut a horse in half and kept on going, coming to rest sticking halfway through a wall of a warehouse. People came running from all over town to see what had happened.

A pickpocket had a field day relieving the on-lookers of anything and everything he could. He even took a pocket watch belonging to the mayor.

It didn't take long for THE ADAMS to go down along with her passengers, crew and everything she had on board. To this day, nothing has ever been recovered. Of course, by now, most, if not all of her cargo, would be part of the river. The silverware, silver tea service, etc., as well as the bag of gold Paul was to use for personal expenses and to keep the store going for the first year would still be there, even if the bag is gone. So anytime you pass the Oquawka area, look out across the river and remember THE ADAMS. If you go look-ing, you might be the lucky one to find what is left of her cargo.

CHAPTER XII

NAUVOO

en years of religious conflict followed the Mormons who entered Missouri in the mid 1830's. An order was issued by the governor of Missouri resulting in their explusion from the state.

The Mormons did not move immediately, but when it seemed that it was either leave or be killed, they crossed the Mississippi River and started another settlement at Nauvoo, Illinois.

They found peace there for awhile, but their days in Illinois were numbered. Their leader, Joseph Smith, was a very controversial individual. Because of their belief in polygamy, Smith and his followers received a very hateful reception from the people of Illinois. Many tales of skirmishes and fighting have been recorded. Cruel, and perhaps, unjust treatment followed the Mormon people everywhere.

In the summer of 1844, Joseph Smith and his brother, Hiram, were arrested and thrown in jail in the nearby town of Carthage.

Among the charges placed against the two were thievery and counterfeiting. Both men were to die here, but there are conflicting accounts of exactly what happened.

One account says that Joseph Smith died when he jumped from a second story window at the jail in an effort to escape from an angry mob about to storm the jail.

The most popular and most believed account says that both Smith and his brother were shot and killed right there in the jail by the angry mob who had overpowered the guards and forced their way in.

During this time of trials and tribulations, many families were known to have hidden their money and valuables for fear they would be stolen. These things were put into sealed containers and either dropped into wells or buried. Others felt that nearly all these folks were forced to leave before having the time to retrieve their stashes.

Legend also has it that the elders of the church may have buried many thousands of dollars worth of gold, silver and jewelry under one of their buildings, which is assumed to be the old temple building. Research  into the old city records and plat maps may reveal some clues to the exact location.

Public opinion against the Mormons made it very unwise for any of them to return to the city to find the fortunes left behind after their flight to Utah.

CHAPTER XIII

THE MAID OF IOWA

he first steamboat known to have been built in the state of Iowa was christened THE MAID OF IOWA, and was launched July 27, 1842. The construction site was on the bank of the Skunk River, near the settlement of Augusta, a sleepy little town about eight miles west of the mouth of the Skunk River in southeast Iowa.

The boat was built for Joseph Smith by two men, Levi Moffatt and Captain Dan Jones. The boat measured one hundred fifteen feet from stem to stern and eighteen feet across the center beam and had a payload of just under one hundred tons.

Her maiden voyage, the one and only she made on the Skunk River, had Captain Daniel M. Repshell at the helm.

It is not known just how long Captain Repshell commanded THE MAID, but sometime prior to 1851, the captain's duties were turned over to an experienced riverboat captain by the name of Bill Phelps, who had earlier, in 1837, commanded the steamboat, PAVILION. He is also known to have commanded the steamboat, CONESTOGA, as late as 1861.

She made many trips up and down the Mississippi

River, but her most fateful voyage was a trip up
the Des Moines River in the early 1850's during
the Great Flood.

It had rained for nearly two weeks, dumping
seventy-five inches of rain into the steams and
rivers. The only means of transportation was by
boat. One traveler needing lodging at a river hotel,
the Hotel Manning, in Keosauqua, paddled a row
boat to the hotel and tied it to the second floor
balcony and entered through the window.

The high water mark and the date have been painted on the outside wall of the hotel and are still visible today.

With Captain Phelps, one of the boldest, swashbuckling navigators of his time at the wheel, they started THE MAID'S fateful trip up the Des Moines River.

On deck was a heavy keg of gold coins thought to be the payroll for a company located somewhere along the river. The keg is guessed to have weighed about one hundred fifty pounds and because of its weight, was not carried to the lower deck storeroom.

Legend has it, that on that dark, cloudy night in Van Buren County, captain and crew were said to have engaged in a wild and free drinking party on board. Captain Phelps declared himself unfit to remain in charge and turned the wheel over to his trusted pilot. He told him to keep her straight ahead until he came to an island, then take her up the left side, so as to stay in the main channel of the river. The river was at its greatest floodline and there was nothing but water to be seen.

The pilot saw what he assumed to be the island and swung THE MAID to the left as instructed. They had gone only about an eighth of a mile before the limbs of the cottonwood trees began striking the boat's smoke stacks. Broken limbs showered down on the deck and one large limb swept the keg of gold overboard.

The limb crashed against the stacks with such force that it woke the sleeping captain. About half dressed and in a somewhat dazed condition, Captain Bill rushed to the upper deck.

Taking in the situation, he exclaimed, "We're up, Soap Creek, by God!"

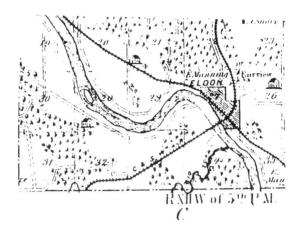

The creek was too narrow to allow the boat to be turned around, therefore, it had to back out of it's difficulty as gracefully as possible. Except for the loss of the gold, the damage was slight and no one was injured.

That expression uttered that night by Captain Bill has been passed down through time and is still used occasionally by the folks yet familiar with the events of that day.

There is no evidence that the gold has ever been recovered from the bottom of Soap Creek. From this point on, there is little, if any, recorded information about the travels of THE MAID OF IOWA or her final resting place.

CHAPTER XIV

THE WONDER OF THE WEST

 he proud and stately queen of the river, called The Wonder Of The West, was THE RUTH. Four decks high, with room for one thousand six hundred passengers, this magnificent side wheeler was equipped with such outlandish and lavish things such as a nursery, laundry, barber shop and a more than adequate-sized bar. Rumor also has it that she was known as the gamblers' special. The money and whiskey flowed as freely as the river.

The main deck of THE RUTH carried twenty five hundred tons of freight, including livestock, cotton, hay and tobacco. The staterooms aboard THE RUTH were described as long rows of little white cottages with marble steps and rosewood doors.

The captain and crew bragged that she was the fastest boat on the river. making the run from New Orleans to St. Louis in the record time of four and a half days, and would triumphantly give three long blasts on her whistle as she entered St. Louis harbor.

Legend also states that THE RUTH was also the runner for large Army payrolls that were supposed to be all in gold coins. The money supposedly was stashed in two wooden forty gallon barrels marked "Pickles" and stored in the hold with the rest of the cargo.

The captains and crews of the riverboats at that time had some very silly superstions, but yet they were very real to them. A white cat was definitely a sign of bad times, but a black cat was absolutely harmless. A coffin with a corpse made a convenient lunch counter or card table, with no bad luck involved.

For over a hundred years, names beginning with

the thirteenth letter of the alphabet, the letter M, were avoided. It was also well known that a white horse or mule brought bad luck to the steamboat, and the thought of having a preacher aboard made some captains very uneasy.

It is said that on one trip in March of 1869 a female passenger by the name of Maggie Mason boarded THE RUTH and that she had her pet white cat hidden in her baggage. On the cargo deck, the two soldiers sent aboard to guard the payroll had also brought aboard a white stallion, as a gift from a prominent general to his wife living in St. Louis.

That fateful day, THE RUTH, mysteriously caught

fire and burned to the water line. Virtually the entire cargo was lost that day.

So somewhere, due to a woman with an unlucky name, or maybe because of a white cat or horse - two pickle kegs full of gold rest on the bottom of the Mississippi River.

CHAPTER XV

THE WOOD LAKE STASH

 he deathbed confession of a Santee Indian Chief called Gray Foot revealed to his sons a tale of robbery and murder.

He told his sons that he had been a member of a band of Santees that had attacked the white agency known as Redwoods in Minnesota. During the raid, many of the soldiers stationed there were killed. After the massacre, the Indians discovered that a large Army payroll, all in gold coins, has been delivered to the post the day before. They found a table in one of the agency buildings heaped with gold coins. Each Indian took a share of the gold with Gray Foot remembering that he had filled a flour sack at least two

thirds full, tied it to his horse, and escaped to the west.

Following the raid, the War Department issued a warning that any Santee Indian caught with gold

in his possession would be automatically considered guilty and would be hanged or face a
military firing squad.

Out of fear for his life, Gray Foot said he had buried
the sack of gold between two straight willow trees
at the east end of Wood Lake in southern
Minnesota.

Gray Foot's loot has
never been found.

CHAPTER XVI

THE WOMAN HATER

orn in October of 1843, one of thirteen children, David Tainter learned to hate all women when he was at an early age. When the Civil War broke out, Tainter was engaged to be married, but he was called off to do his part in fighting the war. While he was gone, his fiancee married another man, thus turning him totally against any and all women for the rest of his life.

Tainter was also an atheist and bore only a grudging tolerance of his fellow man.

After the war, he returned to his home at Prairie du Chien on the Wisconsin River. In 1886, at

the age of 43, Tainter finally found the peace and solitude he wanted on a one-hundred-sixty-acre tract of land in what is known as The Wild Blue Hills.

With his hunting and trapping and a farming background to guide him, Tainter became almost self-sufficent. He raised chickens, had a garden and even kept a few cows. He also had trained dogs that would round up the cows and guard the property. Because he had sworn never to mingle with the outside world, he never left his forest home.

Tainter had supplies delivered to him on a regular basis and he always paid in gold, which people said he seemed to have plenty of.

At least once a year, he sent out a sizable bale of furs along with a bundle of scalps for which he collected bounty money. He had a trusted neighbor

who always handled his business for him and made sure that he had a good supply of rifle shells.

His neighbor estimated that Tainter easily acquired at least a thousand dollars a year from the sale of the furs and that he spent very little for his supplies.

The neighbor's son reported that whenever Tainter needed to pay for something, he would disappear for a few minutes, then return with the exact amount in gold coins. Everyone knew that Tainter was an excellent woodsman and would never hide anything where it could easily be found.

In November of 1917, Tainter committed suicide. He was found dead in his bed with his big toe on the trigger of his rifle and the muzzle propped under his jaw. One of his pet dogs, found lying by the cabin door, had also been shot.

Tainter left an inheritence of eight hundred dollars

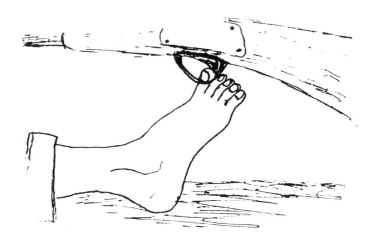

each to several people he knew but not one penny to his only surviving relative, his own brother.

By leaving a will and a sizable amount of money for the authorities to find upon his death, he had finally conformed to society's demands.

But perhaps the most tantalizing thought is speculating on the location of the rest of Tainter's fortune. It is believed that Tainter had put together a fortune of nearly thirty thousand dollars in gold and had buried or hidden it somewhere near his home. The estimated value of that much money in gold coins, on today's market, is much, much more than that.

Being as anti-social as he was, he probably died happy, knowing that his gold was safely buried. To this day, not one ounce of that gold has ever been recovered.

CHAPTER XVII

DUBUQUE'S ECCENTRIC BACHELOR

 he city of Dubuque, Iowa, was named after a wiry, black-haired man by the name of Julien Dubuque. He was the first permanent white settler in Iowa who traveled into the Wisconsin territory to seek his fortune.

He soon learned that the Fox Indians worked several valuable lead deposits on the western side of the Mississippi.

Sometime later, Dubuque had gained the respect and friendship of the tribe and they gave him permission to work those lead deposits also.

He built a settlement and carried on a thriving trade in pig lead and furs.

In September of 1832, an eccentric bachelor lead miner by the name of Thomas Kelly also struck it rich in the lead mines. Kelly converted his large profits into gold. This man was alleged to have buried several large stashes of gold in the area now known as Kelly's Bluff near Dubuque.

Immediately after Kelly's death in 1867, fortune hunters began digging all over the bluff in search of the buried gold.

At first, the city authorities chased the people away trying to keep the bluff and its hidden treasure safe.

But as time passed, sums of $500, $1,200, $1,800, and even $10,000 in gold were uncovered. The

remaining sum of Thomas Kelly's fortune,
estimated at around $200,000, still remains buried
in Kelly's Bluff.

CHAPTER XVIII

THE FARMER'S DAUGHTER

I n the spring of 1925, county authorities were called to the Mattrick farm near Beaver, Wisconsin.

Upon their arrival, they found two dozen men digging in various places around the buildings. The diggers were being protected by a group of excited farmers armed with shotguns.

Further investigation revealed that they were searching for some $11,200 that the farmer's daughter had stolen the year before. They believed she had buried a large share of the loot on the farm and only a small part of it had been recovered.

The daughter had been arrested the previous fall in St. Paul, Minnesota. When she was brought to trial, she pled guilty to larceny and was sentenced to five years in prison.

During the trial, she admitted to stealing the money and burying part of it on her father's farm and stashing the rest at her home in St. Paul.

They recovered $3,000 from the farm but only a small amount from the daughter's home. There was still several thousand dollars missing, and the woman would give no hint as to its location. Many believe the remainder of the money is still buried on the farm and still unrecovered.

CHAPTER XIX

THE ISLAND TREASURE

n 1835, a very well-to-do bachelor bought himself an island sanctuary. The island, just off the Wisconsin shore of the Mississippi, was his own private domain where he lived like a hermit for many years. The old man very seldom spoke to anyone and was generally very tight-lipped about his personal affairs. He did, however, have one weakness. He loved to drink. When under the influence of a fifth or two, he would brag to anyone within shouting distance that his "Good old yella boys" would see to it that he would be very comfortable during his retirement.

"Yellow boys," as everyone knew, was the term he used to refer to the stash of gold that he had hidden somewhere on the island.

Eventually the old man's affair with the whiskey bottle caught up with him. An unknown friend, who came by to visit, found him sprawled in the dirt next to his chicken coop, sloppy drunk and nearly dead from a bullet wound in the chest. He regained consciousness just long enough to yell out a man's name. The name he cried out turned out to be that of the justice of the peace from a nearby settlement. The justice was quickly summoned to the island, but the old man died before the justice got there.

It was everybody's opinion that the murderer had not made off with the man's gold.

For several years thereafter, fortune hunters, outlaws, river pirates, and scores of others, dug all over the island looking for the gold. With their shovels and picks, they dug everywhere; all around the house, in, under and around the chicken coop and even under the flooring of the house.

But, to this day, not one gold coin has ever been known to be recovered from the island.

May he and his gold rest in peace.

CHAPTER XX

THE CLIFF HANGER

round 1825 a keelboat, its captain and crew made their way slowly down the Wisconsin River. Their destination was Fort Crawford at the river settlement of Prairie du Chien.

Stowed on board, along with the rest of her cargo, was an ironbound chest filled with gold, silver, and valuable jewelry.

While unloading, a few supplies at a small river dock, the captain was informed by an Army scout that he and his crew were in danger of being ambushed by a band of hostile Indians known to be in the area.

After unloading the supplies and taking the warning very seriously, they continued on downriver a ways, then again put the boat ashore.

The captain instructed his men to find a safe place to hide the chest until the danger of the Indian attack was over. The men selected a small cave on a rocky bluff overlooking a very secluded section of the river. The entrance to the cave was just below a clearly visible overhang that marked the spot. The opening was then covered with some large rocks and dirt.

Feeling confident that they had safely hidden the chest, they continued their trip down the river.

Strange as it may seem, the rest of the trip to Fort Crawford was quiet and relatively uneventful.

Upon arriving at Prairie de Chien, the captain was only too happy to report that they hadn't seen hide or feather of any Indians.

Several months later, they returned to retrieve the chest from its hiding place. Much to their dismay, as they neared what they thought to be the right location, the place just didn't look the same. Maybe this wasn't the place.

Then one of the men yelled out, "Yes, it is. There's the trail marker I left cut into the side of that tree."

Sure enough, this was the place, but why did it look so different?

"I see why," exclained the captain. "The overhang above the cave is gone and so is half of the cliff."

A terrible storm had passed through the area early in the spring and had dumped several inches of rain. It is speculated that the overhang, now weakened by the torrential rain, had suddenly collapsed and taken half the cliff down with it, thus covering the cave entrance with tons of mud and rock.

Armed with only picks and shovels, the men began digging away at the hillside. They returned to the place several times, digging here and there, but to no avail. All attempts to recover the chest were miserable failures.

Where the overhang once was, the treasure chest still is.

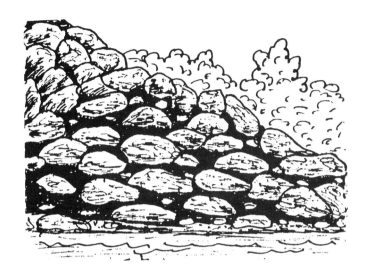

CHAPTER XXI

GRAY LEAD TO YELLOW GOLD

uite some time ago, an elderly Frenchman and his wife lived on an eighty-acre farm near Plattesville, Wisconsin. In his younger years, the Frenchman had mined lead in addition to his farming operation. He was a hard-working man and had amassed a sizable fortune in gold.

His friends constantly encouraged him to put his money in a bank where it would be safe, but his

only reply was, "The best place to keep your money is in your own soil."

He took a large earthen crock, filled it with a fortune in gold coins and buried it on his property known as East Mound.

It is said that the man's wife was the only other person who knew the exact location of the buried

treasure, and they both took the secret to the grave with them. Since the wife evidently had no use for any more than she already had after the death of her husband, she never had a need to dig up the crock of gold, even though he had passed on several years before.

They had no children or family to inherit the gold; and as far as anyone knows, the crock of gold has never been unearthed.

CHAPTER XXII

DISASTER OF '49

 cores of steamboats, sporting their new paint and polish, lined the levee at St. Louis harbor. It was the night of May 17, 1849, and the steward of the paddle wheeler, WHITE CLOUD, was airing sheets, mattresses, and other bedding on the hurricane deck.

Legend has it that a passing steamer, whose identity's unknown, had a minor boiler explosion, which sent sparks and burning embers belching

from her smoke stacks. The sparks raining down on the WHITE CLOUD set the mattresses afire, and soon the entire boat was engulfed in flames.

A strong wind that night, quickly carried the flames to the UDORA and THE EDWARD BATES, lying along side. It wasn't long before the BATES burned loose from her moorings and was set adrift. By that time, she was a floating inferno and spread fire to every boat she touched. Flames lit up the midnight sky, and sparks and embers rained down on the entire waterfront.

Fire raced up and down the harbor, spreading to other boats including THE MONTAUK and THE AMERICAN EAGLE of the Upper Mississippi Fleet, THE ALEXANDER HAMILTON, THE KIT CARSON and THE MANDAN of the Missouri Fleet.

The New Orleans Fleet lost three steamers: THE

BELLE ISLE, THE SARAH and THE MAME LUKE. There were also several Illinois boats involved, including THE ARADIA and THE PRAIRIE STATE.

Two towboats, THE FROLIC and THE GENERAL BROOKS, were also destroyed that fateful night.

When the sun came up in the smoky sky, twenty-seven charred wrecks were strewn along the St. Louis harbor.

It is rumored that hundreds of thousands, and perhaps as much as a million, dollars worth of gold, silver, valuable jewels and other riches too numerous to mention were lost during the disaster and are perhaps still buried beneath the Mississippi mud of St. Louis Harbor.

CHAPTER XXIII

INDIAN JIM

ndian Jim had been banished from his tribe forever for having killed another Indian in a fight. It is believed that Jim was a member of a tribe of Sac Indians that had made an encampment several miles west of the

Skunk River area on the Des Moines River in southeast Iowa.

Indian Jim had a cabin on the south side of Skunk River, a short distance from the town of Lowell, Iowa. Jim shared the cabin with a black man known to everyone only as Mr. Friend. Some didn't believe that his real last name was Friend and that he may have been a former slave who had escaped from some plantation down south.

Down river from Lowell, on the Lee County side of the old Bridgeport Bridge, was a trading post. Jim was a frequent visitor at the trading post where he bought all his supplies. He used small quantities of lead, from a sizable deposit he had found in the area, as money.

In those days, around the mid 1800's, lead was quite valuable and was used in the manufacture of bullets and other products.

Whenever Jim came in with lead for trade, his clothes were always wet. It was thought by the people of the area that the lead deposit was either in the river itself or somewhere near it. Further speculations was that Jim was either crossing the river just to get to the post, or he was deliberately using his wet clothes to throw people off the track and keep them away from the right spot.

Several attempts were made by various people in the area to follow Jim in the hopes that he would, unknowingly, lead them to his lead deposit. He led them on many a wild-goose chase and they all came up empty-handed.

One day Indian Jim decided to return to his village for a visit. Up to this time, he had never disclosed the location of his find to anyone. The day before he returned to the village he decided to show Mr. Friend exactly where the lead deposit was, but when he arrived at the cabin, he found Friend a bit under the weather and unable to go with him to see the lead.

Jim then told Friend that he would show him where the lead was when he returned from the village.

Indian Jim never returned. He was killed by a vengeful family member of the man he had killed. The location of the lead deposit was never revealed.

Some seventy-five years later, two hunters crossing a creek near the Skunk River, accidently discovered an unusual mineral deposit. Not knowing exactly

what he had found, one of the hunters took a sample of the ore to town to have it examined. The sample proved to be a very high-quality lead.

The find was made near a brushy, snake-infested area about three quarters of a mile up river from the trading post known as Hell's Hollow.

The men returned to the area several times; but as far as anyone knows, the lead deposit has never been found.

Has Indian Jim taken the secret location to the grave with him? It seems that he has.

CHAPTER XXIV

DOUBLE OR NOTHING

n the early 1800's several forts and stockades were built along the Mississippi River in western Illinois. The forts were there to give refuge and protection to the people of the area in the event of Indian attack, something that happened all too often.

One such fort was that of John Hill located just outside the town of Carlyle, in Clinton County.

It was reported, by those who knew him, that before his death in 1833, John buried a large hoard of gold in or near the fort. It is also believed that the secret of the exact location went to the grave with Hill, as there is no record of the cache ever being recovered.

Treasure hunters also take heart in the local legend that says that a settler named Young was killed in an Indian attack and buried near the fort. His mother declared that she had sewn the tidy sum of $5,000 into the pockets of his clothing at the time of his burial. Dedicated attempts have been made to find the unmarked grave and claim the contents, but all have turned up nothing.

As far as we know, Hill and Young, or the ghosts thereof, still guard the treasures of Fort Hill.

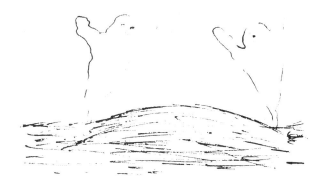

CHAPTER XXV

THE GOLD DOWN UNDER

rom a little Illinois town, right there where Coon Creek empties into the Mississippi, comes the allegedly true story of a wealthy merchant, Frank Barron, and the gold down under.

By the late 1800's Frank had made a sizable fortune in gold. He had no faith or trust in bankers

or banks, so he kept his fortune in gold hidden.

Also through this time, Frank and his wife, Sarah, had a very stormy relationship. It got so bad that their only means of communication was either through a third party or by leaving each other notes. If he left a note

asking for something particular for dinner, for example, stew, he always got something else, like hash, just out of spite. He finally made up his mind that Sarah would never get one penny of his fortune.

About this time, it was decided that a new outhouse was needed. Frank began digging the pit and before he had finished, it was several feet deeper than he really needed it. By dark of night, Frank buried his gold in the bottom of the pit and covered it over with a layer of cement. The outhouse was then finished with no one the wiser.

A couple of years later, Frank found out he had a serious heart problem and had only a short time to live. He then decided to tell his doctor, Dr. Abel Thomas, about the buried gold, as the doctor was a man he felt he could trust.

Dr. Thomas was to inherit the gold, only after Sarah had also passed away. The agreement was made and not long after, Frank died.

Sarah frantically searched everywhere for the gold but never found it.

Dr. Thomas anxiously awaited the call to come and attend to Sarah. The call never came and Sarah seemed to be getting stronger and living better with each passing year.

Several years went by and Dr. Thomas's health began to fail. By this time, Dr. Thomas's son, George, had also become a doctor and would be taking the older doctor's place when he passed on.

Taking George aside one day, Dr. Thomas told him about the buried fortune in gold. The same agreement was made that George could go after the gold after Sarah passed away.

Several months later, Dr. Thomas died. Now Dr. George was left to watch and wait for the fateful day, but Sarah continued to enjoy amazingly good health.

Several years had passed, when suddenly Dr. George suffered a sudden stroke and died.

Three years later, Sarah finally passed away without ever finding Frank's fortune.

With the advent of indoor plumbing, the outhouses slowly disappeared, one by one. The town slowly grew and prospered. New homes were built, the streets were paved, and most everything else seemed to get covered up.

To this day, the gold still lies buried somewhere down under.

EPILOGUE

Many secrets have grown out of the passions and ambitions of the men and women who have worked, lived and loved along the banks of The Great Mississippi.

Some of these secrets lie yet buried in the waters and in the black soil of its banks and those of its tributaries.

Fortunes in gold, volumes of trash, fine jewelry and foolish junk all lie yet buried where secreted by fire, storms and fear many years ago.

Since you have enjoyed this book, perhaps you would be interested in some of these others from QUIXOTE PRESS.

ARKANSAS BOOKS

HOW TO TALK ARKANSAS
     by Bruce Carlson .... paperback $7.95
ARKANSAS' ROADKILL COOKBOOK
     by Bruce Carlson .... paperback $7.95
REVENGE OF ROADKILL
     by Bruce Carlson .... paperback $7.95
GHOSTS OF THE OZARKS
     by Bruce Carlson .... paperback $9.95
A FIELD GUIDE TO SMALL ARKANSAS FEMALES
     by Bruce Carlson .... paperback $9.95
LET'S US GO DOWN TO THE RIVER 'N...
     by various authors .... paperback $9.95
ARKANSAS' VANISHING OUTHOUSE
     by Bruce Carlson .... paperback $9.95
TALL TALES OF THE MISSISSIPPI RIVER
     by Dan Titus .... paperback $9.95
LOST & BURIED TREASURE OF THE MISSISSIPPI RIVER
     by Netha Bell & Gary Scholl .... paperback $9.95
TALES OF HACKETT'S CREEK
     by Dan Titus .... paperback $9.95
UNSOLVED MYSTERIES OF THE MISSISSIPPI RIVER
     by Netha Bell .... paperback $9.95
101 WAYS TO USE A DEAD RIVER FLY
     by Bruce Carlson .... paperback $7.95
VACANT LOT, SCHOOL YARD & BACK ALLEY GAMES
     by various authors .... paperback $9.95
HOW TO TALK MIDWESTERN
     by Robert Thomas .... paperback $7.95
ARKANSAS COOKIN'
     by Bruce Carlson .... (3x5) paperback $5.95

DAKOTA BOOKS

HOW TO TALK DAKOTA .... paperback $7.95
Some Pretty Tame, but Kinda Funny Stories About Early
DAKOTA LADIES-OF-THE-EVENING
     by Bruce Carlson .... paperback $9.95

(133)

SOUTH DAKOTA ROADKILL COOKBOOK
by Bruce Carlson .... paperback $7.95
REVENGE OF ROADKILL
by Bruce Carlson .... paperback $7.95
101 WAYS TO USE A DEAD RIVER FLY
by Bruce Carlson .... paperback $7.95
LET'S US GO DOWN TO THE RIVER 'N...
by various authors .... paperback $9.95
LOST & BURIED TREASURE OF THE MISSOURI RIVER
by Netha Bell .... paperback $9.95
MAKIN' DO IN SOUTH DAKOTA
by various authors .... paperback $9.95
GUNSHOOTIN', WHISKEY DRINKIN', GIRL CHASIN' STORIES
OUT OF THE OLD DAKOTAS
by Netha Bell .... paperback $9.95
THE DAKOTAS' VANISHING OUTHOUSE
by Bruce Carlson .... paperback $9.95
VACANT LOT, SCHOOL YARD & BACK ALLEY GAMES
by various authors .... paperback $9.95
HOW TO TALK MIDWESTERN
by Robert Thomas .... paperback $7.95
DAKOTA COOKIN'
by Bruce Carlson .... (3x5) paperback $5.95

ILLINOIS BOOKS

ILLINOIS COOKIN'
by Bruce Carlson .... (3x5) paperback $5.95
THE VANISHING OUTHOUSE OF ILLINOIS
by Bruce Carlson .... paperback $9.95
A FIELD GUIDE TO ILLINOIS' CRITTERS
by Bruce Carlson .... paperback $7.95
YOU KNOW YOU'RE IN ILLINOIS WHEN...
by Bruce Carlson .... paperback $7.95
Some Pretty Tame, but Kinda Funny Stories About Early
ILLINOIS LADIES-OF-THE-EVENING
by Bruce Carlson .... paperback $9.95
ILLINOIS' ROADKILL COOKBOOK
by Bruce Carlson .... paperback $7.95
101 WAYS TO USE A DEAD RIVER FLY
by Bruce Carlson .... paperback $7.95

HOW TO TALK ILLINOIS

    by Netha Bell .... paperback $7.95

TALL TALES OF THE MISSISSIPPI RIVER

    by Dan Titus .... paperback $9.95

TALES OF HACKETT'S CREEK

    by Dan Titus .... paperback $9.95

UNSOLVED MYSTERIES OF THE MISSISSIPPI

    by Netha Bell .... paperback $9.95

LOST & BURIED TREASURE OF THE MISSISSIPPI RIVER

    by Netha Bell & Gary Scholl .... paperback $9.95

STRANGE FOLKS ALONG THE MISSISSIPPI

    by Pat Wallace .... paperback $9.95

LET'S US GO DOWN TO THE RIVER 'N...

    by various authors .... paperback $9.95

MISSISSIPPI RIVER PO' FOLK

    by Pat Wallace .... paperback $9.95

GHOSTS OF THE MISSISSIPPI RIVER (from Keokuk to St. Louis)

    by Bruce Carlson .... paperback $9.95

GHOSTS OF THE MISSISSIPPI RIVER (from Dubuque to Keokuk)

    by Bruce Carlson .... paperback $9.95

MAKIN' DO IN ILLINOIS

    by various authors .... paperback $9.95

MY VERY FIRST

    by various authors .... paperback $9.95

VACANT LOT, SCHOOL YARD & BACK ALLEY GAMES

    by various authors .... paperback $9.95

HOW TO TALK MIDWESTERN

    by Robert Thomas .... paperback $7.95

INDIANA BOOKS

HOW TO TALK INDIANA .... paperback $7.95

INDIANA'S ROADKILL COOKBOOK

    by Bruce Carlson .... paperback $7.95

REVENGE OF ROADKILL

    by Bruce Carlson .... paperback $7.95

A FIELD GUIDE TO SMALL INDIANA FEMALES

    by Bruce Carlson .... paperback $9.95

GHOSTS OF THE OHIO RIVER (from Cincinnati to Louisville)

    by Bruce Carlson .... paperback $9.95

LET'S US GO DOWN TO THE RIVER 'N...

    by various authors .... paperback $9.95

101 WAYS TO USE A DEAD RIVER FLY
  by Bruce Carlson .... paperback $7.95
INDIANA'S VARNISHING OUTHOUSE
  by Bruce Carlson .... paperback $9.95
VACANT LOT, SCHOOL YARD & BACK ALLEY GAMES
  by various authors .... paperback $9.95
HOW TO TALK MIDWESTERN
  by Robert Thomas .... paperback $7.95

IOWA BOOKS

IOWA COOKIN'
  by Bruce Carlson .... (3x5) paperback $5.95
IOWA'S ROADKILL COOKBOOK
  By Bruce Carlson .... paperback $7.95
REVENGE OF ROADKILL
  by Bruce Carlson .... paperback $7.95
IOWA'S OLD SCHOOLHOUSES
  by Carole Turner Johnston .... paperback $9.95
GHOSTS OF THE AMANA COLONIES
  by Lori Erickson .... paperback $9.95
GHOSTS OF THE IOWA GREAT LAKES
  by Bruce Carlson .... paperback $9.95
GHOSTS OF THE MISSISSIPPI RIVER (from Dubuque to Keokuk)
  by Bruce Carlson .... paperback $9.95
GHOSTS OF THE MISSISSIPPI RIVER (from Minneapolis to Dubuque)
  by Bruce Carlson .... paperback $9.95
GHOSTS OF POLK COUNTY, IOWA
  by Tom Welch .... paperback $9.95
TALES OF HACKETT'S CREEK
  by Dan Titus .... paperback $9.95
ME 'N WESLEY (stories about the homemade toys that
 Iowa farm children made and played with around the turn of the century)
  by Bruce Carlson .... paperback $9.95
TALL TALES OF THE MISSISSIPPI RIVER
  by Dan Titus .... paperback $9.95
HOW TO TALK IOWA .... paperback $7.95
UNSOLVED MYSTERIES OF THE MISSISSIPPI
  by Netha Bell .... paperback $9.95
101 WAYS TO USE A DEAD RIVER FLY
  by Bruce Carlson .... paperback $7.95

LET'S US GO DOWN TO THE RIVER 'N...
    by various authors .... paperback $9.95
TRICKS WE PLAYED IN IOWA
    by various authors .... paperback $9.95
IOWA, THE LAND BETWEEN THE VOWELS
  (farm boy stories from the early 1900s)
    by Bruce Carlson .... paperback $9.95
LOST & BURIED TREASURE OF THE MISSISSIPPI RIVER
    by Netha Bell & Gary Scholl .... paperback $9.95
Some Pretty Tame, but Kinda Funny Stories About Early
IOWA LADIES-OF-THE-EVENING
    by Bruce Carlson .... paperback $9.95
THE VANISHING OUTHOUSE OF IOWA
    by Bruce Carlson .... paperback $9.95
IOWA'S EARLY HOME REMEDIES
    by 26 students at Wapello Elem. School .... paperback $9.95
IOWA - A JOURNEY IN A PROMISED LAND
    by Kathy Yoder .... paperback $16.95
LOST & BURIED TREASURE OF THE MISSOURI RIVER
    by Netha Bell .... paperback $9.95
FIELD GUIDE TO IOWA'S CRITTERS
    by Bruce Carlson .... paperback $7.95
OLD IOWA HOUSES, YOUNG LOVES
    by Bruce Carlson .... paperback $9.95
SKUNK RIVER ANTHOLOGY
    by Gene Olson .... paperback $9.95
VACANT LOT, SCHOOL YARD & BACK ALLEY GAMES
    by various authors .... paperback $9.95
HOW TO TALK MIDWESTERN
    by Robert Thomas .... paperback $7.95

KANSAS BOOKS

HOW TO TALK KANSAS .... paperback $7.95
STOPOVER IN KANSAS
    by Jon McAlpin .... paperback $9.95
LET'S US GO DOWN TO THE RIVER 'N ...
    by various authors .... paperback $9.95
LOST & BURIED TREASURE OF THE MISSOURI RIVER
    by Netha Bell .... paperback $9.95

101 WAYS TO USE A DEAD RIVER FLY
     by Bruce Carlson .... paperback $7.95
VACANT LOT, SCHOOL YARD & BACK ALLEY GAMES
     by various authors .... paperback $9.95
HOW TO TALK MIDWESTERN
     by Robert Thomas .... paperback $7.95

KENTUCKY BOOKS

GHOSTS OF THE OHIO RIVER (from Pittsburgh to Cincinnati)
     by Bruce Carlson .... paperback $9.95
GHOSTS OF THE OHIO RIVER (from Cincinnati to Louisville)
     by Bruce Carlson .... paperback $9.95
TALES OF HACKETT'S CREEK
     by Dan Titus .... paperback $9.95
LOST & BURIED TREASURE OF THE MISSISSIPPI RIVER
     by Netha Bell & Gary Scholl .... paperback $9.95
LET'S US GO DOWN TO THE RIVER 'N ...
     by various authors .... paperback $9.95
UNSOLVED MYSTERIES OF THE MISSISSIPPI
     by Netha Bell .... paperback $9.95
101 WAYS TO USE A DEAD RIVER FLY
     by Bruce Carlson .... paperback $7.95
TALL TALES OF THE MISSISSIPPI RIVER
     by Dan Titus .... paperback $9.95
MY VERY FIRST
     by various authors .... paperback $9.95
VACANT LOT, SCHOOL YARD & BACK ALLEY GAMES
     by various authors .... paperback $9.95

MICHIGAN BOOKS

MICHIGAN COOKIN'
     by Bruce Carlson .... (3x5) paperback $5.95
MICHIGAN'S ROADKILL COOKBOOK
     by Bruce Carlson .... paperback $7.95
MICHIGAN'S VANISHING OUTHOUSE
     by Bruce Carlson .... paperback $9.95

MINNESOTA BOOKS

MINNESOTA'S ROADKILL COOKBOOK
by Bruce Carlson .... paperback $7.95
REVENGE OF ROADKILL
by Bruce Carlson .... paperback $7.95
A FIELD GUIDE TO SMALL MINNESOTA FEMALES
by Bruce Carlson .... paperback $9.95
GHOSTS OF THE MISSISSIPPI RIVER (from Minneapolis to Dubuque)
by Bruce Carlson .... paperback $9.95
LAKES COUNTRY COOKBOOK
by Bruce Carlson .... paperback $11.95
UNSOLVED MYSTERIES OF THE MISSISSIPPI
by Netha Bell .... paperback $9.95
TALES OF HACKETT'S CREEK
by Dan Titus .... paperback $9.95
GHOSTS OF SOUTHWEST MINNESOTA
by Ruth Hein .... paperback $9.95
HOW TO TALK LIKE A MINNESOTA NATIVE .... paperback $7.95
MINNESOTA'S VANISHING OUTHOUSE
by Bruce Carlson .... paperback $9.95
TALL TALES OF THE MISSISSIPPI RIVER
by Dan Titus .... paperback $9.95
Some Pretty Tame, but Kinda Funny Stories About Early
MINNESOTA LADIES-OF-THE-EVENING
by Bruce Carlson .... paperback $9.95
101 WAYS TO USE A DEAD RIVER FLY .... paperback $7.95
LOST & BURIED TREASURE OF THE MISSISSIPPI RIVER
by Netha Bell & Gary Scholl .... paperback $9.95
VACANT LOT, SCHOOL YARD & BACK ALLEY GAMES
by various authors .... paperback $9.95
HOW TO TALK MIDWESTERN
by Robert Thomas .... paperback $7.95
MINNESOTA COOKIN'
by Bruce Carlson .... (3x5) paperback $5.95

MISSOURI BOOKS

MISSOURI COOKIN'
by Bruce Carlson .... (3x5) paperback $5.95
MISSOURI'S ROADKILL COOKBOOK
by Bruce Carlson .... paperback $7.95

REVENGE OF ROADKILL
by Bruce Carlson .... paperback $7.95
LET'S US GO DOWN TO THE RIVER 'N ...
by various authors .... paperback $9.95
LAKES COUNTRY COOKBOOK
by Bruce Carlson .... paperback $11.95
101 WAYS TO USE A DEAD RIVER FLY
by Bruce Carlson .... paperback $7.95
TALL TALES OF THE MISSISSIPPI RIVER
by Dan Titus .... paperback $9.95
TALES OF HACKETT'S CREEK
by Dan Titus .... paperback $9.95
STRANGE FOLKS ALONG THE MISSISSIPPI
by Pat Wallace .... paperback $9.95
LOST & BURIED TREASURE OF THE MISSOURI RIVER
by Netha Bell .... paperback $9.95
HOW TO TALK MISSOURIAN
by Bruce Carlson .... paperback $7.95
VACANT LOT, SCHOOL YARD & BACK ALLEY GAMES
by various authors .... paperback $9.95
HOW TO TALK MIDWESTERN
by Robert Thomas .... paperback $7.95
UNSOLVED MYSTERIES OF THE MISSISSIPPI
by Netha Bell .... paperback $9.95
LOST & BURIED TREASURE OF THE MISSISSIPPI RIVER
by Netha Bell & Gary Scholl .... paperback $9.95
MISSISSIPPI RIVER PO' FOLK
by Pat Wallace .... paperback $9.95
Some Pretty Tame, but Kinda Funny Stories About Early
MISSOURI LADIES-OF-THE-EVENING
by Bruce Carlson .... paperback $9.95
GUNSHOOTIN', WHISKEY DRINKIN', GIRL CHASIN'
STORIES OUT OF THE OLD MISSOURI TERRITORY
by Bruce Carlson .... paperback $9.95
THE VANISHING OUTHOUSE OF MISSOURI
by Bruce Carlson .... paperback $9.95
A FIELD GUIDE TO MISSOURI'S CRITTERS
by Bruce Carlson .... paperback $7.95
EARLY MISSOURI HOME REMEDIES
by various authors .... paperback $9.95
GHOSTS OF THE OZARKS
by Bruce Carlson .... paperback $9.95

MISSISSIPPI RIVER COOKIN' BOOK
        by Bruce Carlson .... paperback $11.95
MISSOURI'S OLD HOUSES, AND NEW LOVES
        by Bruce Carlson .... paperback $9.95
UNDERGROUND MISSOURI
        by Bruce Carlson .... paperback $9.95

NEBRASKA BOOKS

LOST & BURIED TREASURE OF THE MISSOURI RIVER
        by Netha Bell .... paperback $9.95
101 WAYS TO USE A DEAD RIVER FLY
        by Bruce Carlson .... paperback $7.95
LET'S US GO DOWN TO THE RIVER 'N ...
        by various authors .... paperback $9.95
HOW TO TALK MIDWESTERN
        by Robert Thomas .... paperback $7.95
VACANT LOT, SCHOOL YARD & BACK ALLEY GAMES
        by various authors .... paperback $9.95

TENNESSEE BOOKS

TALES OF HACKETT'S CREED
        by Dan Titus .... paperback $9.95
TALL TALES OF THE MISSISSIPPI RIVER
        by Dan Titus .... paperback $9.95
UNSOLVED MYSTERIES OF THE MISSISSIPPI
        by Netha Bell .... paperback $9.95
LOST & BURIED TREASURE OF THE MISSISSIPPI RIVER
        by Netha Bell & Gary Scholl .... paperback $9.95
LET'S US GO DOWN TO THE RIVER 'N ...
        by various authors .... paperback $9.95
101 WAYS TO USE A DEAD RIVER FLY
        by Bruce Carlson .... paperback $7.95
VACANT LOT, SCHOOL YARD & BACK ALLEY GAMES
        by various authors .... paperback $9.95

HOW TO TALK WISCONSIN .... paperback $7.95
WISCONSIN COOKIN'
      by Bruce Carlson .... (3x5) paperback $5.95
WISCONSIN'S ROADKILL COOKBOOK
      by Bruce Carlson .... paperback $7.95
REVENGE OF ROADKILL
      by Bruce Carlson .... paperback $7.95
TALL TALES OF THE MISSISSIPPI RIVER
      by Dan Titus .... paperback $9.95
LAKES COUNTRY COOKBOOK
      by Bruce Carlson .... paperback $11.95
TALES OF HACKETT'S CREEK
      by Dan Titus .... paperback $9.95
LET'S US GO DOWN TO THE RIVER 'N ...
      by various authors ....paperback $9.95
101 WAYS TO USE A DEAD RIVER FLY
      by Bruce Carlson...paperback $7.95
UNSOLVED MYSTERIES OF THE MISSISSIPPI
      by Netha Bell .... paperback $9.95
LOST & BURIED TREASURE OF THE MISSISSIPPI RIVER
      by Netha Bell & Gary Scholl .... paperback $9.95
GHOSTS OF THE MISSISSIPPI RIVER (from Dubuque to Keokuk)
      by Bruce Carlson .... paperback $9.95
HOW TO TALK MIDWESTERN
      by Robert Thomas .... paperback $7.95
VACANT LOT, SCHOOL YARD & BACK ALLEY GAMES
      by various authors .... paperback $9.95
MY VERY FIRST
      by various authors ....paperback $9.95
EARLY WISCONSIN HOME REMEDIES
      by various authors .... paperback $9.95
GHOSTS OF THE MISSISSIPPI RIVER (from Minneapolis to Dubuque)
      by Bruce Carlson ....paperback $9.95
THE VANISHING OUTHOUSE OF WISCONSIN
      by Bruce Carlson .... paperback $9.95
GHOSTS OF DOOR COUNTY, WISCONSIN
      by Geri Rider .... paperback $9.95
Some Pretty Tame, but Kinda Funny Stories About Early
WISCONSIN LADIES-OF-THE-EVENING
      by Bruce Carlson .... paperback $9.95

MIDWESTERN BOOKS

A FIELD GUIDE TO THE MIDWEST'S WORST RESTAURANTS
    by Bruce Carlson .... paperback $5.95
THE MOTORIST'S FIELD GUIDE TO MIDWESTERN FARM
EQUIPMENT (misguided information as only a city slicker can give it)
    by Bruce Carlson .... paperback $5.95
VACANT LOT, SCHOOL YARD & BACK ALLEY GAMES
OF THE MIDWEST YEARS AGO
    by various authors .... paperback $9.95
MIDWEST SMALL TOWN COOKING
    by Bruce Carlson .... (3x5) paperback $5.95
HITCHHIKING THE UPPER MIDWEST
    by Bruce Carlson .... paperback $7.95
101 WAYS FOR MIDWESTERNERS TO "DO IN" THEIR
NEIGHBOR'S PESKY DOG WITHOUT GETTING CAUGHT
    by Bruce Carlson .... paperback $5.95

RIVER BOOKS

ON THE SHOULDERS OF A GIANT
    by M. Cody and D. Walker .... paperback $9.95
SKUNK RIVER ANTHOLOGY
    by Gene "Will" Olson .... paperback $9.95
JACK KING vs. DETECTIVE MACKENZIE
    by Netha Bell .... paperback $9.95
LOST & BURIED TREASURES ALONG THE MISSISSIPPI
    by Netha Bell & Gary Scholl .... paperback $9.95
MISSISSIPPI RIVER PO' FOLK
    by Pat Wallace .... paperback $9.95
STRANGE FOLKS ALONG THE MISSISSIPPI
    by Pat Wallace .... paperback $9.95
GHOSTS OF THE OHIO RIVER (from Pittsburgh to Cincinnati)
    by Bruce Carlson .... paperback $9.95
GHOSTS OF THE OHIO RIVER (from Cincinnati to Louisville)
    by Bruce Carlson .... paperback $9.95
GHOSTS OF THE MISSISSIPPI RIVER (Minneapolis to Dubuque)
    by Bruce Carlson .... paperback $9.95
GHOSTS OF THE MISSISSIPPI RIVER (Dubuque to Keokuk)
    by Bruce Carlson .... paperback $9.95
TALL TALES OF THE MISSISSIPPI RIVER
    by Dan Titus .... paperback $9.95

TALL TALES OF THE MISSOURI RIVER
    by Dan Titus .... paperback $9.95
RIVER SHARKS & SHENANIGANS
  (tales of riverboat gambling of years ago)
    by Netha Bell .... paperback $9.95
UNSOLVED MYSTERIES OF THE MISSISSIPPI
    by Netha Bell .... paperback $9.95
TALES OF HACKETT'S CREEK (1940s Mississippi River kids)
    by Dan Titus .... paperback $9.95
101 WAYS TO USE A DEAD RIVER FLY
    by Bruce Carlson .... paperback $7.95
LET'S US GO DOWN TO THE RIVER 'N ...
    by various authors .... paperback $9.95
LOST & BURIED TREASURE OF THE MISSOURI
    by Netha Bell .... paperback $9.95

COOKBOOKS

ROARING 20's COOKBOOK
    by Bruce Carlson .... paperback $11.95
DEPRESSION COOKBOOK
    by Bruce Carlson .... paperback $11.95
LAKES COUNTRY COOKBOOK
    by Bruce Carlson .... paperback $11.95
A COOKBOOK FOR THEM WHAT AIN'T DONE A LOT OF COOKIN'
    by Bruce Carlson .... paperback $11.95
FLAT-OUT DIRT-CHEAP COOKIN' COOKBOOK
    by Bruce Carlson .... paperback $11.95
APHRODISIAC COOKING
    by Bruce Carlson .... paperback $11.95
WILD CRITTER COOKBOOK
    by Bruce Carlson .... paperback $11.95
I GOT FUNNIER-THINGS-TO-DO-THAN-COOKIN' COOKBOOK
    by Louise Lum .... paperback $11.95
MISSISSIPPI RIVER COOKIN' BOOK
    by Bruce Carlson .... paperback $11.95
HUNTING IN THE NUDE COOKBOOK
    by Bruce Carlson .... paperback $9.95
DAKOTA COOKIN'
    by Bruce Carlson .... (3x5) paperback $5.95
IOWA COOKIN'
    by Bruce Carlson .... (3x5) paperback $5.95

MICHIGAN COOKIN'
by Bruce Carlson .... (3x5) paperback $5.95
MINNESOTA COOKIN'
by Bruce Carlson .... (3x5) paperback $5.95
MISSOURI COOKIN'
by Bruce Carlson .... (3x5) paperback $5.95
ILLINOIS COOKIN'
by Bruce Carlson .... (3x5) paperback $5.95
WISCONSIN COOKIN'
by Bruce Carlson .... (3x5) paperback $5.95
HILL COUNTRY COOKIN'
by Bruce Carlson .... (3x5) paperback $5.95
MIDWEST SMALL TOWN COOKIN'
by Bruce Carlson .... (3x5) paperback $5.95
APHRODISIAC COOKIN'
by Bruce Carlson .... (3x5) paperback $5.95
PREGNANT LADY COOKIN'
by Bruce Carlson .... (3x5) paperback $5.95
GOOD COOKIN' FROM THE PLAIN PEOPLE
by Bruce Carlson .... (3x5) paperback $5.95
WORKING GIRL COOKING
by Bruce Carlson .... (3x5) paperback $5.95
COOKING FOR ONE
by Barb Layton .... paperback $11.95
SUPER SIMPLE COOKING
by Barb Layton .... (3x5) paperback $5.95
OFF TO COLLEGE COOKBOOK
by Barb Layton .... (3x5) paperback $5.95
COOKING WITH THINGS THAT GO SPLASH
by Bruce Carlson .... (3x5) paperback $5.95
COOKING WITH THINGS THAT GO MOO
by Bruce Carlson .... (3x5) paperback $5.95
COOKING WITH SPIRITS
by Bruce Carlson .... (3x5) paperback $5.95
INDIAN COOKING COOKBOOK
by Bruce Carlson .... paperback $9.95
DIAL-A-DREAM COOKBOOK
by Bruce Carlson .... (3x5) paperback $5.95
HORMONE HELPER COOKBOOK .... (3x5) paperback $5.95

MISCELLANEOUS BOOKS

DEAR TABBY (letters to and from a feline advice columnist)
by Bruce Carlson .... paperback $5.95
HOW TO BEHAVE (etiquette advice for non-traditional
and awkward circumstances such as attending dogfights,
what to do when your blind date turns out to be your spouse, etc.)
by Bruce Carlson .... paperback $5.95
REVENGE OF THE ROADKILL
by Bruce Carlson .... paperback $7.95

(146)

INDEX

(Chapter titles are in capital letters.)

INDEX

154

Need a Gift?

For

- Shower • Birthday • Mother's Day •
  • Anniversary • Christmas •

Turn Page For Order Form
(Order Now While Supply Lasts!)

TO ORDER COPIES OF

LOST AND BURIED TREASURE OF THE MISSISSIPPI RIVER

Please send me_____copies of **Lost and Buried Treasure of the Mississippi River** at $9.95 each. (Make checks payable to **QUIXOTE PRESS**.)

Name _____

Street _____

City _____ State _____ Zip Code _____

SEND ORDERS TO:

QUIXOTE PRESS
31798 K18S
Sioux City, IA 51109

TO ORDER COPIES OF

LOST AND BURIED TREASURE OF THE MISSISSIPPI RIVER

Please send me_____copies of **Lost and Buried Treasure of the Mississippi River** at $9.95 each. (Make checks payable to **QUIXOTE PRESS**.)

Name _____

Street _____

City _____ State _____ Zip Code _____

SEND ORDERS TO:

QUIXOTE PRESS
31798 K18S
Sioux City, IA 51109